Copyright © 2019 SuperSummary

All rights reserved. No part of this publication may be reproduced, transmitted, or distributed in any form, by electronic or mechanical means, including photocopying, scanning, recording, or file sharing, without prior permission in writing from the publisher, except as provided by United States of America copyright law.

The purpose of this study guide is to provide supplemental educational material. It is not intended as a substitute or replacement of THE LAND OF OPEN GRAVES.

Published by SuperSummary, www.supersummary.com

ISBN – 9781074414474

For more information or to learn about our complete library of study guides, please visit http://www.supersummary.com

Please submit any comments, corrections, or questions to: http://www.supersummary.com/support/

TABLE OF CONTENTS

PLOT OVERVIEW	2
CHAPTER SUMMARIES AND ANALYSES	5
Introduction-Chapter 3	5
Chapters 4-7	15
Chapters 8-12	27
CHARACTER ANALYSIS	41

Jason De León
Mike Wells
Memo
Lucho
Maricela (Carmita Maricel Zhagüi Puyas)
José Tacuri
Christian

THEMES	49
SYMBOLS AND MOTIFS	55
IMPORTANT QUOTES	59
ESSAY TOPICS	70

PLOT OVERVIEW

The Land of Open Graves: Living and Dying on the Migrant Trail is a 2015 work of nonfiction and the winner of four awards, including the J.J. Staley Book Prize in 2018. Drawing on his expertise in anthropology, ethnography and archeology, author Jason De León, Executive Director of the Undocumented Migration Project and current Professor of Anthropology and Chicano/a Studies at the University of California, Los Angeles, critiques the federal border enforcement policy known as Prevention Through Deterrence.

From the outset of his book, De León argues that Prevention Through Deterrence, the policy that claims to use the "'inhospitable'" conditions of the Sonora Desert, between Arizona and Mexico, as a means of preventing illegal immigration, has in actuality "set the stage for the desert to become the new 'victimizer' of border transgressors" (34; 35). De León states that the policy, which has been in effect since the mid-1990s, uses nature as a foil to disguise the "hybrid collectif of deterrence" that incorporates the federal government's own responsibility for migrant deaths (60).

De León opens his book with his first day of ethnographic research in Nogales, Mexico, during which he sees the body of a migrant who has perished in the desert. This visceral image of a corpse being left to the flies leads into De León's manifesto, which seeks to expose the "innumerable consequences" the sociopolitical phenomenon of Prevention Through Deterrence has for "the lives and bodies of undocumented people" (4).

The primary section of De León's book, "Dangerous Ground," discusses the policy of Prevention Through

Deterrence and the role of human and non-human actors in relation to the policy. Through expeditions that include a journey looking for migrant remains in the desert, and using the bodies of freshly-killed pigs to assess the rate of decomposition, De León brings the reader into close contact with the violence that migrants experience and the way federal border policy uses the desert to do its "dirty work" (68).

Part 2, "El Camino," introduces the reader to Memo and Lucho, two repeat border-crossers De León meets at the migrant shelter Albergue Juan Bosco in Nogales, Mexico. The ensuing chapters follow the two men's experiences of the cycle of attempted crossing, deportation, and preparing to cross again. De León accompanies Memo and Lucho to the grocery store, where they buy $26 worth of provisions for their journey through the Sonora Desert. He then visits the US Border Patrol's billion-dollar collection of detection "gadgets" and notes the disparity in cost and technical sophistication between the migrants' preparation and that of Border Patrol (155). Nevertheless, De León shows that between 92 and 98% of those attempting to cross into the US eventually do make it across the border, as with each failed attempt they gain greater knowledge of the desert and develop new technologies of their own.

In the final part of the book, "Perilous Terrain," De León recounts the journey taken from finding a woman's rotting corpse in the desert to tracing her identity and learning how her family responded to her loss. He presents a shocking sense of the disparity between Border Patrol and the family's perceptions of the victim, Ecuadorian Carmita Maricela Zhagüi Puyas, who goes by Maricela. Whereas Border Patrol viewed Maricela as part of the illegal migrant body count, her family, both near and extended, continue to feel her loss, which their lives have been irrevocably changed by it.

De León then goes to show, through the case of José Tacuri, the trauma faced by families who were not able to recover the body of a loved one who disappeared in the desert. He thus exposes how the policy of Prevention Through Deterrence, which allows migrants to try their luck at crossing a deadly landscape, has consequences not only for the individual, but for their entire family and community.

De León concludes by asking the reader to empathize with the migrants whose stories animate his book and to fully recognize their humanity, rather than dismissing them as illegals whose lives do not matter because they have transgressed border law. He admits that there is no easy solution for the problem of undocumented migration but suggests fairer economic policies between the United States and its neighbors, so that fewer migrants feel that their home countries are devoid of opportunity and that they have no choice but to make the perilous journey of entering the United States illegally.

CHAPTER SUMMARIES AND ANALYSES

Introduction-Chapter 3

Introduction Summary

The subject of Jason De León's book is "the violence and death that border crossers face on a daily basis as they attempt to enter the United States without authorization by walking across the vast Sonoran Desert of Arizona" (3). Those who successfully cross the border do the backbreaking essential jobs that United States citizens are themselves reluctant to do, such as meat processing and fruit-picking. Many of those crossing the desert have made several attempts to do so, as their lives fall into a pattern of illegal border crossing and deportation. In 2013 alone, nearly 2 million illegal migrants were removed from the country. A large proportion of deportees are now "running scared across Arizona's Mars-like landscape" as they seek ways to return to their families and homes (3).

De León's argument is that the death, disfigurement, and sexual abuse that migrating people experience en route "are neither random nor senseless, but part of a strategic federal plan," a "killing machine that simultaneously uses and hides behind the viciousness of the Sonora Desert" (3-4). As a result, Border Patrol seeks to redirect blame onto the natural landscape and "render invisible" the innumerable consequences that migration and deportation have for the migrants involved (4). In writing his book, De León seeks to give voice to these underrepresented people and keep track of their different trajectories.

From a historical perspective, the book's subject begins in 1993, when the policy of "'Prevention Through Deterrence (PTD)'" was utilized for the first time in El Paso, Texas

(5). The policy's popularity increased and between 2000 and 2013, 4,584,022 of the 11.7 million people arrested for crossing the border illegally were apprehended in the Tucson Sector, "a craggy, depopulated and mountainous patch of land that stretches westward from New Mexico to the Yuma County line in Arizona" (6).

The horrors described in De León's book take place in a part of the desert that lies south of Tucson, between the Baboquivari and Tumacácori mountains, which have been home to the indigenous Tohono O'odham (desert people) for thousands of years. "What's agonizing for the O'odham" De León writes, "is that the American federal government has turned their sacred landscape into a killing field, a massive open grave" (8).

De León's study of desert migration began as a dinner conversation with an archeologist friend in the fall of 2008, when De León was fresh out of graduate school. His friend told him how he stumbled on objects that migrants had left behind as he undertook archeological surveys in the Arizona desert. One such object was a love letter, written in Spanish, which read in part: "'I bet someone could do some sort of weird archeological project'" on the fate of migrants in the desert (10). A month later, De León found himself standing in the wilderness south of Tucson, staring at the discarded artifacts.

He began the Undocumented Migration Project (UMP) in 2009, intending to test the idea that archeology could enhance understanding of how border-crossing technology had evolved over the years, along with the economic system that underpins illegal migration.

De León considers that to date, the covert nature of undocumented migration has meant that academics have generally studied the phenomenon from a distance. The problem with Leo Chavez's *Shadowed Lives* and David Spener's *Clandestine Crossings,* De León contends, is that they were written after the crossing happened and were exclusively based on interviews. Medical anthropologist Seth Holmes, who wrote *Fresh Fruit, Broken Bodies* accompanied migrants who were crossing the border in the Sonora Desert. De León considers that Holmes's efforts focus too much on his own experiences as a white researcher and thus diminish the real trauma faced by his companions. Rather, in his own approach to the topic of clandestine migration, De León has "sought to paint crossers not as anonymous shadows scrambling through the desert, but as real people who routinely live and die in this environment and whose voices and experiences we should be privileging" (13). A Latino, De León conducts his interviews with the people he talks to on the road in Spanish and while he edits them, he tries to remain faithful to his interviewees' tone of voice.

Chapter 1 Summary: "Prevention Through Deterrence"

De León, along with his photographer, Mike Wells, and their guide, Bob Kee, are on the hunt for skeletal remains of border crossers in the Sonora desert. When Kee had encountered a skeleton a few weeks earlier, the police quickly became unmotivated by the heat and reinforced that looking for the remains of a dead illegal immigrant was not a priority for them.
De León considers that the label "'illegal'" is all too convenient for US citizens, who wish to discredit the legitimacy of migrants in order to "avoid speaking their names or imagining their faces" (26). These citizens have also suffered "historical amnesia" and thereby forgotten that theirs is a country of immigrants, where groups such as

the Irish and Chinese were once unwelcome (26). De León argues that "disregard for the lives of undocumented people and the idea that dead bodies should act as a deterrence to future migrants" is part of the federal government's border security plan (27).

De León considers that the border fits in to Giorgio Agamben's theory of the "state of exception [...] the process whereby sovereign authorities declare emergencies in order to suspend the legal protections afforded to individuals while simultaneously unleashing the power of the state on them" (27). The Sonora desert border is one such zone, as officials do not recognize unauthorized migrants' civil rights. De León considers that "the isolation of the desert, combined with the public perception of the border as a zone ruled by chaos, allows the government to justify using extraordinary measures to control and exclude 'uncivilized' non-citizens" (28).

The corpses of 2,721 unauthorized migrants were recovered between October 2000 and September 2014 in southern Arizona. About 800 of these bodies remain unidentified. In 2012, De León noticed the American Department of Homeland Security's sign in the men's bathroom, which was written in Spanish and read: "'[T]he next time you try to cross the border without documents you could end up a victim of the desert'" (29). De León found it interesting that the desert was personified as an entity capable of inflicting violence on migrants, and how the sign ignored the strategic relationship between federal border enforcement policy and the Sonora desert's deadly natural setting.

De León writes that "[r]ather than shooting people as they jumped the fence, Prevention Through Deterrence set the stage for the desert to become the new "'victimizer of border transgressors'" (35). According to Department of Homeland Security figures, the numbers of known migrant deaths rose from 250 in 1999 to 492 in 2005; however, De León suspects that the Federal Government "lowballs these body counts" and hypothesizes that between 2000 and 2014, there were "enough corpses to fill the seats on fifty-four Greyhound buses," though the actual number of victims will be forever unknown (36).

Chapter 2 Summary: "Dangerous Ground"

It has been 20 years since Border Patrol Sector Chief Silvestre Reyes lined up agents along the banks of the Rio Grande to stop border crossers from scaling the fence and running into downtown El Paso. This set off the chain reaction that gave rise to Prevention Through Deterrence. De León argues that the moniker Prevention Through Deterrence "wants to convince you that it's a policy designed simply to prevent crime, to discourage it before it happens" (38). De León contends that the violence set in motion by Prevention Through Deterrence is extensive and unpredictable.

De León says that to comprehend how agency is constructed, our analytical gaze must widen to include all of the components—human, animal, and meteorological—and not pander to the overly-simple idea that the desert is a "ruthless beast that law enforcement cannot be responsible for" (43). De León seeks to redress this wrong by focusing his ethnographic lens on migrant experience, thus beginning to add a graphic reality to federal policy discourse. De León stages a semi-fictionalized ethnography, which according to Humphreys and Watson's definition is "'a restructuring of events occurring within one or more ethnographic investigations into a single narrative'" (43). This aims to bring readers closer to the reality of migrant experiences.

De León's ethnography begins with nine strangers in a hotel in Nogales, Mexico where five border-crossers have gone to rest before their passage into the desert. One of the nine, Javier, has given $400 to a people-smuggler as a down payment. Another, Lupe, fantasizes about being reunited with her children when she makes the crossing. A woman called La Güera drives the nine up to the Sonora Desert's wide expanse. On their trek through the desert, the nine face tribulations such as extreme dehydration—they resort to drinking their own urine—and an encounter with *bajadores*, desert bandits, who demand the crossers' IDs and money and that the group strip naked. The *bajadores* abuse Lupe. After this, Javier, Marcos, Lupe and Carlos keep moving, while the rest of the group decide to return and report themselves to border control.

De León concludes that "labelling migrant deaths an act of nature" is a convenient way to "ignore the hybrid collectif of deterrence that was initially set in motion by policy strategists 20 years ago and that continues to function today" (60).

Chapter 3 Summary: "Necroviolence"

In 2012, De León staged an experiment where three juvenile female pigs were killed and dressed in clothes similar to those worn by migrants. The animals' decomposition process was then monitored. The pigs were used in place of migrants in what Kirskey and Helmreich call a "multispecies ethnography; that is, an ethnography that focuses on how the lives and deaths of humans and nonhumans are closely intertwined and jointly shaped by cultural, economic, and political forces" (64). A similar experiment was performed in 2013 with two adult male pigs, where one was covered with a pile of rocks and brush, mimicking an ad hoc burial, and the other placed near a large tree. In this instance, the speed of decomposition and the manner in which carrion-eaters fed off the bodies was measured. De León aims to show how "the hybrid collectif of border enforcement has set the stage for scavenging animals to come into close and (from a human perspective) violent contact with the bodies of hundreds of border crossers a year" (64).

De León's pig experiment is a study of necropolitics, or killing in the name of sovereignty, whereby a nation decides which lives are valuable, and who may live and who must die. Necroviolence is the name De León gives to the "specific treatment of corpses that is perceived to be offensive, sacrilegious, or inhumane" by perpetrators, victims and their cultural group (69). He also argues that the lack of a body, which has been eaten or has disappeared, allows the perpetrators, Border Patrol, and the government "plausible deniability," while provoking trauma among mourners, who cannot go through a natural process of grieving (71).

De León's placement of a dead pig near a tree in the 2013 experiment mimics the practice of border-crossers who feel that they are approaching death and have the impulse to get away from the light. These shade-seekers are often found dead after being "rotisserie-cooked by the rotating sun" (74). The pigs by the tree went through the "'fresh'" early stages of body decomposition: discoloring, swelling, and being attacked by maggots before carrion-eaters could get to them (75).

In five days, the turkey vultures—carrion-eaters, with an impressive wingspan—arrive. They devour the flesh in stages and keep coming even when the viscera and muscle have been consumed. By the end, the migrant-dressed pig is reduced to "a mummified skin suit with the red bra still attached" (79). Skeletal remains are collected 50 meters from their original location.

At a bunk in the Juan Bosco shelter, an old man is traumatized by the loss of his wife, who died in the desert. The group that the couple was traveling with had to leave her body behind. A man called Patricio tells De León that migrants who die on the trail are often covered with rocks, so that vultures cannot reach them. However, on the migrant trail, there is no proper burial that fits in with the majority of migrants' Roman Catholic faith. Worse of all, when the body is absent, it is virtually impossible to hold a wake and pray for the deceased's soul. A destroyed or incomplete corpse may negatively affect the afterlife for the deceased, according to Roman Catholic theology, as it may stop the deceased from rising from the dead to be judged at the appointed time.

From a practical standpoint, the absent body destroys evidence that the person was there in the first place, and means that the total number of migrant deaths is ultimately unknown. De León considers that this lets the government somewhat off the hook, and that the carrion-eaten, disappeared bodies "are logical extensions of a political process," which contributes to their use of the desert as a form of deterrence (84).

Introduction-Chapter 3 Analysis

In the opening chapters of his book, De León shows how Border Patrol and the government are using the Sonora desert as a form of controlling illegal immigration on the US-Mexico border. While the government argues that the harsh natural conditions of the desert act as a deterrent for illegal crossings, De León refuses to let America wash its hands of its culpability, because illegal immigrants who are successful in crossing this border are those who do essential work that Americans will not do. Moreover, following the North American Free Trade Act of 1994, "the United States promised economic prosperity for its southern neighbor if it would only open up its ports of entry and take shipment of cheap goodies" (6). The influx of "*gringo* corn" into Mexico decimated the country's agriculture and put millions of peasant farmers out of work, meaning that their only chance for prosperity was to scale the border (6).

America justifies the harrowing occurrences in the Sonora desert—which include death by dehydration and predation by bandits and carrion-eaters—by emphasizing that the crossers are illegal and so should not be there anyway. De León shows how the American media's persistent focus on the immigrants' illegality is a way of stripping away their humanity. Further, this focus on illegality proactively ignores the fact that people are suffering brutal deaths on American soil.

Seeking to re-humanize these illegals, De León uses a number of ethnographic techniques. First, looking for the remains of migrants who have died on the trail, De León experiences the harsh conditions of the desert for himself, finding himself "periodically shivering and getting dizzy; [his] body is working hard to make sense of this inferno" (24). By subjecting himself to the desert and the resulting bodily trauma, De León shows that his own, privileged researcher's body has the same make-up as anyone attempting to cross the border. Using visceral, corporeal imagery to describe his experience, De León diminishes the distance between himself, the reader, and the migrants.

In Chapter 2's semi-fictionalized ethnography, an overall impression inspired by a collation of interviews, De León tries to "match the frankness, sarcasm, and humor of [his] interlocutors, as well as the grittiness of the difficult worlds they inhabit" (14). This is evident when the nine fictionalized migrants swear and tease each other, using Spanish colloquialisms. In addition to humor, De León evokes pathos in the case of Lupe, a woman who wishes to be reunited with her children and undergoes sexual abuse at the hands of the *bajadores*. De León's description of how a *bajador* "squeezes one of her brown breasts like he is testing the ripeness of some fruit" both exoticizes and objectifies Lupe, in addition to illustrating her extreme vulnerability as a young woman in the lawless land of the desert (53).

Finally, in staging the multi-species ethnography, where dead, clothed pigs stand in for migrant corpses, De León monitors the rate and stages of decomposition of bodies on the trail. Imitating the habit of dying migrants to choose the shade of a tree for their final breaths, De León places his pig in a similar place. He describes how the shade cannot last, due to the ruthlessness of the rotating sun. Both the migrant and pig corpses are later carried off by carrion-eaters, their bodies dispersed up to fifty meters from the site of their death (74). De León juxtaposes his multi-species ethnography with a real-life tale of an old man grieving his wife. The woman died under a tree beside the trail, without a proper Roman Catholic burial, as would have been desired. The migrants' "'bad death'" in the desert, which De León defines as a death that "occurs in the wrong place and at the wrong time" further underscores his point that the government and Border Control are trying to use the harsh natural conditions in the desert as not only a deterrent for illegal immigration, but as a means of ending lives that they consider less important than American ones (82).

Chapters 4-7

Chapter 4 Summary: "Memo and Lucho"

De León met Memo and Lucho, who are male, uneducated and fairly typical of the migrants who try to cross the border, at the Albergue Juan Bosco in July 2009, after they had been deported. The Albergue is a place where De León conducted many of his interviews and would also volunteer. There, he learned how deportees are treated by the media, humanitarian groups, and other agencies.

De León believes that these border-crossing men's *chingaderas*—Mexican "'play routines'" that are laden with humor, expletives and sexually-charged double entendres—are important, because this "humor reflects an understanding of people's own precarious social positions and at times functions as 'a weapon of the weak' as migrants discursively resist the power of the US federal government to stop them from crossing" (89; 92). As a Latino male from a working-class background, border-crossers respond to De León in a more natural, unfiltered manner than his white, middle-class counterparts.

The men, who were "*amigos de camino*" had crossed the US-Mexico border illegally multiple times, with Memo making fifteen crossings (94). Both Memo and Lucho were determined to cross the border at any cost, feeling that there was nothing for them in Mexico. While Memo has family back in Veracruz, he does not want to go back there unless he has some money for them; that he has not been able to make a success of himself, and has returned to Mexico penniless on previous occasions, is a source of shame to him. Lucho has his trailer, two cars, a girlfriend, and family in the United States, and feels that there is truly nothing for him in Mexico.

De León writes that "one of the major misconceptions about immigration control is that if the government spends enough money on fences, drone planes, motion sensors, and Border Patrol agents and makes the crossing process treacherous enough, people will eventually stop coming" (101). However, nearly two decades of research has shown that these boundary enforcements play little role in deterring people from crossing the border. Regardless of the difficulty of the crossing, about 92-98% of all people attempting to cross the border eventually get through to the US, though they can be found out and deported when they are pulled over by the police for minor infringements of the law, such as driving offences. Memo and Lucho are well aware of the dangers that face them in crossing the border, but are still determined to go ahead with it because of the fact that "it is a lot harder to live in Mexico than the US," because in Mexico, the cost of living is higher in comparison with wages (103).

Chapter 5 Summary: "Deported"

At a deportation center in Nogales, De León writes that "as immigration control has ratcheted up […] so too has the use of deportation as a routinised disciplinary method critical to the maintenance of state sovereignty around the world" (108). Although deportation is an essential element of the social process of undocumented migration into the United States, there has been little ethnographic work focusing on what it looks like, how it's experienced, and its relationship to other aspects of border crossing. De León provides "snapshots of the steps, settings, and actors involved in the deportation process in Southern Arizona and Northern

Mexico to demonstrate how this phenomenon is both a bureaucratic and physical component of the hybrid collectif" that Prevention by Deterrence and the use of the desert as a scapegoat enables (108-09).

Whereas in the decades leading up to the immigration reforms of the mid-2000s, illegal immigrants were typically returned over the border with minimal processing, in a procedure known as voluntary departure, now there is a stricter policy in place, called "enforcement with consequences" (109). This often results in a game of "catch and release" between Border Patrol and immigrants who try to cross the border as many times as their courage permits them to (109). However, since 2005, the Department of Homeland Security began experimenting with new types of deportation procedures, such as court-hearings and prison sentences. For example, a repeat offender can find themselves charged with felony reentry, which "generally carries a two-year maximum penalty or up to twenty years in prison if the defendant has a criminal record" (110). A procedure known as Operation Streamline, which aims to catch migrants out, takes place five days a week in California, Arizona, and Texas. However, given that the federal courthouses can often only process a maximum of 70 cases a day, it is a matter of luck as to whether detainees will appear before a judge. Most who are tried will receive a sentence of up to 180 days, though the average time detained is 30 days.

In order to discourage deportees from returning and making a second attempt to cross the border, Border Patrol drops them off at a port of entry distant from where they made their crossing attempt. De León contends that this practice is less about disrupting human traffickers or protecting people than it is about "disorienting deportees and literally placing them in harm's way" (115). Whereas finding a coyote (a person whose job it is to smuggle people) from one's own town is the safest option for a second attempt at crossing the border:

> [B]y sending people to a foreign border town and disconnecting them from a smuggler with whom they may have had some social tie, the Border Patrol simultaneously places people in a geographically hostile environment and encourages them to contract an unfamiliar smuggler who is more likely to rob them than help them cross over (115).

The narrow strip of land along the border wall with the Grupo Beta Office and where deportees usually end up is called *la linea* by migrants. De León considers it a scene of infinite human variety. It is full of recently-deported migrants who are eager to retry their luck. Then there is the common story of families being split up, and on either side of the border. De León says how in the Obama era of mass deportations, the phrase "'I have to see my kids' has become a campaign slogan for determined deportees" (125).

Given the hardships on *la linea*, "a place where you can get robbed by the police, kidnapped by smugglers, hassled by local gangs, or assaulted by the mescal-chugging hoodlums who live in the municipal cemetery next to the basketball court," friendships both genuine and of convenience emerge (135). There are also angels "of mercy" such as Chuco, who walks up and down *la linea*, handing out water, toothbrushes, and razors to migrants. Life is especially difficult for women, who are prone to assault, false promises of their relatives being found in exchange for sexual favors, and an inability to work and gather sufficient funds for their crossing due to childcare responsibilities.

De León concludes that *la linea* is a place characterized by cyclical movement, of people attempting to make a crossing, being apprehended, and trying again. He concludes that "the complexities of the post-deportation world can rival what people experience in the desert or can be far worse" (143).

Chapter 6 Summary: "Technological Warfare"

De León's friends, Memo and Lucho, tell him they are going to cross the border and do a preparatory shopping trip at the grocery store, in anticipation of their harsh journey through the desert. The cost of the supplies comes to $26, which does not seem like much in US money, but owing to the high cost of living in Mexico, where a pizza costs as much as a day's wages, they have had to work for whole weeks before they have sufficient funds to make the crossing. As they pack, Memo and Lucho continue to crack jokes, brandishing a tiny toy gun for scaring away desert animals. Still, De León is concerned that owing to the number of calories they will burn in the desert, they will only have sufficient food for four days. It is an emotional goodbye for De León when his two friends head to the desert.

Whereas Memo and Lucho spent only $26 dollars preparing for their illegal crossing, their rivals, the Border Patrol agents, are equipped with billions of dollars' worth of boundary enforcements. On a tour of the Border Patrol headquarters, De León was especially impressed by an assault rifle, which "can fire 750 rounds a minute and has a muzzle velocity of 950 meters per second" (154). Nevertheless, despite the disparity between the crossers' meager technology for crossing the desert and the Border Patrol's high-tech provisions, the crossers "routinely find new and inventive ways" to get through (156).

At the time that De León was writing his book, 351 miles of the 1,954-mile border that existed between the United States and Mexico were walled. De León considers that:

> [D]espite the evidence that the border wall is no match for catapults, car jacks and other forms of human ingenuity, the United States can't seem to shake the fixation that building more of it will somehow solve many of our country's economic and social problems (156).

The wall is a fixation of conservative politicians; for example, on his 2011 election campaign, Republican candidate Herman Cain:

[R]eceived thunderous applause while making the following statement to a crowd in Cookeville, Tennessee, regarding his plans for immigration security: 'we'll have a real fence. Twenty feet high with barbed wire. Electrified with a sign on the other side that says, 'It can kill you'" (156).

De León wonders which laborers Cain would use to build his wall and makes the ironic suggestion of using "the California-based construction firm that was fined in 2006 for hiring undocumented laborers to help build the border wall between Tijuana and San Ysidro" (156).

De León considers that the Border Patrol agents know that walls do not prevent migration and that "the best and most lethal weapon the Border Patrol has is nature" (158). Along some parts of the border, there are no walls, just "a three-strand barbed-wire fence or nothing at all," and in Walker Canyon, "there is even an unlocked gate you can open and close at will" (158). This is all part of Border Patrol's plan, as "catching someone at the moment of entry and deporting them back to Mexico leaves the person relatively fresh and energized to try again right away" (158). They recognize that "it is better to let migrants to go a few rounds with heat stroke, *bajadores*, and whatever else they might encounter in the wilderness" (159). Only "after they have had some licks" do Border Patrol agents hunt people down and march them back to Mexico (159). One candid border agent admitted to anthropologist Rocío Magaña that migrant exhaustion facilitated his ability to deport people. Customs and Border Protection statistics support this trend, as between 2010 and 2011, only 21% of apprehension in the Tucson Sector happened within a mile of the border. The vast majority of those apprehended "spent a significant amount of time experiencing the Sonoran hybrid collectif's choke hold" (160).

On the Mexican side of the border, whole industries have sprung up to make crossing more successful. For one, there are specialized vendors who sell camouflaged backpacks and high salt content food for inflated prices. There is also the knowledge that migrants themselves gain after making several failed attempts: "the trauma induced by extreme dehydration and punishing terrain on a first failed crossing attempt makes for a steep learning curve if you survive" (163). Mexicans joke that for them, there are no borders.

When Memo and Lucho fail at their latest crossing attempt, after they get caught, they sink into a deep, exhausted depression, appearing "ghosts of themselves" (164). After an evening of drink and an impetus to violence, they repeat how they have to cross the border like a mantra.

Chapter 7 Summary: "The Crossing"

De León gets a phone call from Memo and Lucho, who have safely made it into Arizona, though their trailer seems perilously close to the border. When he asks them to recount their journey, it is with the awareness that "the act of remembering can conjure pain, fear, and despair. Among American families with undocumented members, it is not uncommon for the topic of their crossing to be a forbidden subject" (168).

De León outlines Memo and Lucho's final crossing using a combination of interview excerpts and the photographs they took en route. He feels privileged to include their narrative in his work, but considers that it is important to acknowledge these undocumented migrants' stories, because, "like other immigrant groups before them, these Latino families may have to wait one or more generations before reaching a status in US society that allows them to vocalize their migration experiences without trepidation or shame" (168).

Given that these stories may become sanitized over time, De León draws attention to the importance of using an archeological approach in order to examine the abandoned objects that border crossers have left behind. Doing so "can foster engagements with the recent past and its material remains in novel and meaningful ways and produce new information that may be lost in narrative translations of history, collectif memories, or accounts of individual experiences" (172). This "breadcrumb trail of ripped clothes and bone-dry water bottles" is "American immigration history in the making" (170). Anti-immigration activists refer to these discarded objects as "migrant 'trash,'" as though they are symptomatic of what migrants will do once they enter the country (170).

The Undocumented Migration Project has used an archeological approach to create a typology of migrant sites, an analysis of the wear patterns on recovered objects and relative dating techniques that illuminate how the social process of clandestine migration has evolved over time. Coupled with personal testimonies, De León considers that this is the closest we can get to understanding what happens on the migrant trail.

Archeologists on the migrant trail often find it useful to visit *"layups,"* a term used by Border Patrol to describe the places where migrants eat, rest, shade, and hide from law enforcement who may deport them. Archeologists have developed a typology to better analyze these *layups,* which include:

> [C]*ampsites* where people congregate and rest for a period ranging from a few hours to an entire night; *rest sites* where people stop briefly and consume food and beverages; *pickup sites* where migrants dump all of their desert supplies and get picked up by smugglers in vehicles; and *religious shrines* where offerings are left to ensure a safe journey (176).

There are also border-staging areas, where immigrants wait for the right time to cross.

Many of the sites used by border crossers are also employed by drug mules. While the latter tend to leave a lighter archeological footprint, distinguishing between the two groups can be complicated by the fact that some border crossers work as *burreros* to pay for their crossing fees and so appear to be carrying the same equipment. Shoes are especially valuable to archeologists, who want to detect use-wear and the kind of suffering people experience crossing the desert. A pair of abandoned shoes in the desert often indicate someone who was left behind on the migrant trail.

Dating the evidence found on the migrant trail can present a challenge to archeologists. Some of it may be extremely recent, and ephemera such as bus tickets can give precise dates, whereas more relative clues, such as the development of rust on an object, can be more complicated to construct a timeline for. Further:

> [U]nlike ancient sites buried under stratigraphic layers of dirt and gravel, these migrant archeological contexts are alive and dynamic. What is recorded today may drastically change tomorrow as a locale is destroyed through environmental conditions or modified by other people passing through (187).

The reason that so many objects are abandoned on the trail is not, as some racist anti-immigration activists say, because Latinos have insufficient regard for the environment, but rather because their exhausted bodies can no longer withstand the weight of non-essential possessions. Also, at the final stage of movement through the desert, the pickup site—that is, the area where coyotes arrange for vehicle transportation for border crossers—is the place where crossers are forced to clean up their appearance and discard any obvious traces of the desert. During this often-chaotic transformation, crossers can lose valuable personal effects, such as identification cards, photos, and other valuables.

Memo and Lucho consider that they were successful in their crossing because they only crossed in the most remote, most difficult areas, where there were giant rocks and mountains rather than roads and trails. After their crossing, the two men are traumatized, often suffering nightmares and "hitting the bottle hard" (196). Moreover, in 2015, when De León catches up with the two men, more than five years after their journey, he realizes that their "memories of the event and the months spent in Nogales have been affected by the passage of time" (197). Some of this self-editing is conscious, and done as a matter of coping; interestingly, while Memo's retelling is funnier, Lucho's is more reflective. For Memo, the fact that he made the crossing is a point of gratitude and even a feeling that he has been "reborn," but he also has a vision of returning to Mexico when he has enough money to support himself (201).

De León considers that his archeological approach "may also help correct erroneous characterizations of the crossing process that are written by those in power or by those invested in demonizing Latino migrants and distinguishing them from previous generations of 'noble' immigrants" (197). The Latino immigration story also may be lost because of the invisibility of illegal immigrants, who continue to live in Agamben's "'state of exception'" (199): "Immigrants are tolerated when they do the jobs that citizens won't, but the American public has little interest in hearing their voices, preserving their history, or affording them any rights" (199). Given concerted federal and state efforts to clear the desert of migrant traces, there is a high possibility that the story of illegal crossings will be lost. Memo, however, keeps his camouflage backpack as a memento of his journey.

Chapters 4-7 Analysis

"El camino," which translates from Spanish as "the road," and is the title given to Chapters 4-7, does not only refer to the migrants' treacherous trek across the desert but also to the numerous preparations for the journey. These include saving one's meager wages for a few weeks to buy enough provisions for the trip or to secure the assistance of a coyote. It may also include a visit to a specialist store on the Mexican side of the border that sells camouflage backpacks and water bottles. Moreover, there are lengthy waits in deportation centers and deportation rehabilitation centers, where crossers recover from failed attempts to make the journey and regroup their resources, both physical and emotional, in order to try again. As De León shows, the process of crossing the border is often cyclical and can takes months, if not years.

Memo and Lucho, the friends De León makes at the Juan Bosco center for recently deported immigrants in Nogales, are the stars of Chapters 4-7. Becoming friends with these two working-class Mexican men, De León gains both practical and emotional insight into the experience of deportation. De León grows progressively closer to the duo as they deliberate and finally decide when they will make their next crossing. They keep De León on his toes, telling him that they are going to cross the border "very soon," but then keep postponing the departure date (145). Just as De León wonders whether Memo and Lucho will "transition" from border-crossing hopefuls into permanent, Juan Bosco shelter staff, they surprise him by announcing that they will make a shopping trip to buy provisions for their desert crossing (146). De León participates in the joke-telling that attempts at "lightening the mood" and thereby passing over the dangers that the two men will face, though he is seriously worried about their fate and even feels he may start "blubbering" when he sees them off (151; 153). When the duo's expedition ends in deportation, De León is devastated and keeps drinking to drown out the pain and frustration. De León's sustained emotional engagement with the two men draws upon Ruth Behar's comment that "'anthropology that doesn't break your heart just isn't worth doing'" (153). His reactions continually emphasize to the reader that life on the border concerns real human beings and not just statistics.

Nevertheless, De León backs up his description of Memo and Lucho with the fruits of his extensive anthropological study. For example, he can see that Memo and Lucho are traumatized by their crossing and that this affects how they remember the journey, both consciously and subconsciously. De León senses that they only reminisce about the desert for his benefit, while they try to forget the experience for themselves, dismissing it through their usual jokes and having "dreams about walking in the desert or dreams that [they] are being chased" (195).

Moreover, De León quotes the 92-98% success rate of migrants eventually succeeding in crossing the border. This success rate illustrates a visceral determination to cross. In his description of Lucho and Memo, De León shows how after a failed immigration attempt, a drunk, devastated Lucho "starts sobbing and says, 'We have to cross. We have to cross. We have to cross'" (166). Both as individuals and as a collective, De León's picture of both the micro and the macro shows that crossing the border is one that poor Mexicans feel compelled to do, believing that in the US, they will earn higher wages and a better quality of life for their families.

Chapters 8-12

Chapter 8 Summary: "Exposure"

On June 28, 2012, three students associated with the Undocumented Migration Project summer field school spend the day with volunteers from the Tucson Samaritans. Their research goal is to observe the organization's humanitarian efforts and to collect ethnographic and archeological data on food and water depots in the desert. They meet a 19-year-old migrant named Carlos; he is from

El Salvador. Carlos reports that a coyote got frustrated with people who were sick and couldn't go as fast as the coyote wanted them to. He called out that Border Patrol agents were near and everyone scattered. One of the women from the group had been sick and vomiting and Carlos had gone to get help for her. No one caught her name.

When De León walked the trail in 2009, it was full of relics from border-crossers. By 2010, these relics had either been cleaned up or disintegrated in the extreme conditions. On July 2, 2012, De León spontaneously decides to visit the old trail, accompanied by his students. One of De León's students charges ahead of the group and runs back screaming that there is someone up there. It turns out to be the corpse of a woman. They call 911 and report that they have found a body while hiking. De León reminds himself that "directing a research project focused on human suffering and death in the desert means we can't ignore certain parts of the social process just because it sickens us or breaks our hearts" (210). Later, when De León is criticized for taking the pictures of the corpse because he has robbed the woman of her dignity, he claims that it is imperative to "point out that the deaths that migrants experience in the Sonoran Desert are anything but dignified" (213). He gets close to the dead woman's body, takes photos to record exactly what death in desert looks like, and allows space for both himself and his students to feel uncomfortable. De León suspects that the woman, who was lying face down in the dirt, died while tying to get up the hill after she had walked more than 40 miles. As De León and his students wait, they cover the woman's body with a blanket they have found on the trail, thus protecting it from the vultures.

When the Border Patrol agents arrive, there are two young ones—one Mexican-American and one white—

accompanied by a senior officer. The senior officer is experienced in dealing with bodies and refers to the practical aspects of the task, such as "'we gotta roll her over and put her in the bag because she is gonna leak'" (215). The younger white agent makes a joke about how "'gross'" it is to be dealing with a body; De León marvels at the irony of how "Border Patrol routinely refer to living migrants as 'bodies' in everyday discourse, but many of them seem totally unprepared for dealing with the actual dead ones"(216).

Weeks later, Robin Reineke, a cultural anthropologist who works at the Pima County Office of the Medical Examiner, identifies the body as 38-year-old Maricela Ahguipolla, from Guatemala. She is the woman who fell sick in the group that included Carlos from El Salvador.

Chapter 9 Summary: "You Can't Leave them Behind"

In Jackson Heights, Queens, De León meets Christian, the Ecuadorian brother-in-law of Maricela, the body found in the previous chapter. Christian, who left his home country in 2001, as part of the wave of 137,000 Ecuadorian migrants to the United States, sends money home to "support an extended family, to build a house he has never set foot in, and to clothe, feed and educate a son whose hand he has never held" (221). He says he tried to discourage Maricela from emigrating, because he did not want her to undergo the same traumatic experiences as him.

As bad as the border crossing is for Mexicans, for many non-Mexican nationals, it's even worse, because it is a process that can last for weeks or even months. Christian left Ecuador because his family was impoverished and he needed to go to the United States to make enough money to support and educate them. Given that his trip, made on

September 16th or 17th of 2001 was in the wake of 9/11, Carlos thought that he could help clean up the destroyed buildings in New York. He was especially sad about leaving his sister, Vanessa, whom he loved most at the time: "These are the things that leave a mark on you. You can't leave them behind" (224).

The "expensive obstacle course" that non-Mexican migrants have to make through Central America and Mexico before they even get to the border is more dangerous even than what awaits them in the desert (225): "For Central and South Americans, Mexico is its own hybrid collectif of immigration enforcement" (225). The conditions are so dire that many people disappear on this leg of the journey.

Christian crossed the border in a large group, at a time before the post-9/11 escalation in security. Christian got caught by Border Patrol twice and even ended up spending Christmas and New Year's in jail. His uncle hired a lawyer and when he got out of jail, Christian made his way to New York, where his family were. He found that Queens seemed dirty and that he owed $21,000 for the trip, including interest. While Christian's trip is characterized by "high drama," it is typical of the fate of many from Latin America who make their way north (235).

Although Christian has enjoyed good economic opportunities and liberties from being in the United States, he is always conscious of the high personal cost needed to support his family back in Ecuador and "the tension of being caught between two disparate worlds is the source of much pain" for him (236). He fears that he may get found out for being illegal and be deported back to Ecuador, where he may no longer be accustomed to life.

Chapter 10 Summary: "Maricela"

De León goes to visit Maricela's family in Cuenca, Ecuador. They are living in a house that is known as "'Christian's house,'" because he has funded it, even though he has never been there (238). Maricela wanted to build such a house for her own family after she returned from America. De León's visit is a populous one; he is accompanied by his photographer, Mike Wells, and their spouses and children. They are warmly welcomed by Doña Dolores, Maricela's mother-in-law, and Vanessa, Christian's sister and Maricela's sister-in-law. They talk about the trauma they experienced following Maricela's disappearance and death.

De León tells Maricela's story "through the eyes of the relatives who watched her leave, desperately searched for her when she went missing and dealt with the aftermath of her death" (243). The relatives describe how Maricela was vivacious and popular, loving music and dance. She was so happy that she earned the nickname "mariposa," which means butterfly (244). Upon realizing that there were few opportunities for her children in Ecuador, she determined to go to the United States. Her parting words to her mother-in-law were ominous: "'Whatever my destiny is, I must go'" (245). The last the family heard from her was a Facebook message saying she was getting ready to go into the desert.

De León writes that are significantly fewer ethnographic accounts and journalistic data focused on the experiences of female border crossers than male ones. This is due both to a male subject research bias and the fact that women make up less than 15% of the population of undocumented migrants per year. Women are also 2.67 times more likely to die from exposure to the desert than men; this figure leads researchers to hypothesize that chauvinistic smugglers have a tendency to view women as liabilities, and are therefore more likely to abandon them.

When it became evident that Maricela was lost, her family worried about her and solicited help both from the brother, who had paid for her to go, and from the *pasador,* or people smuggler. The family still do not know exactly what happened to Maricela in the desert. However, her brother-in-law, who accompanied her on the trip, said something about Maricela feeling sick and sitting on a rock and then being separated when something happened to startle the group.

It was difficult for Christian to look for Maricela, especially because he was undocumented, spoke little English, and risked being deported himself if he called border control. Also, he would not be able to obtain precise enough information about where she was in the desert: "By design, locating someone in the depths of the [desert] is nearly impossible" (248). Christian tried calling hospitals, jails, and immigration and detention centers in Arizona, but there was still no sign of Maricela.

On July 27, Christian was told that they had found Maricela and forensics wanted information on her fingerprints and other aspects of her identity. The family was devastated to learn that Maricela had died and said they would not believe the fact of her death until they saw her body.

When Maricela's decomposing body was loaded onto a plane in New York City, "Maricela, like many dead border crossers, transformed from being an anonymous subject unrecognized by the state to a documented Ecuadorian citizen accorded rights and privileges by both her native country and the one that sought to exclude her" (251). The family waited in anticipation for Maricela's body and her wake was attended by hundreds of people.

Viewing the body is an important part of mourning for Catholics, because "it is what makes the death real" (253). Maricela's family were no exception. Christian, who had viewed the body in New York, warned the family not to open the casket, because Maricela's body was badly decomposed. Still, the family opened the casket and saw that Maricela's face was gone and her body in "pieces," symbolic of her violent, degrading death in the desert (254).

The family were eager to see the pictures De León had taken of Maricela in the desert. Christian noticed that in De León's photographs, Maricela retained her hands, whereas her corpse was handless. De León speculates that the fingers were cut off to get Maricela's fingerprints. Vanessa, Maricela's sister-in-law, finds the process of looking at De León's photographs helpful: the desert corpse is more recognizably Maricela than the body that was brought to them in pieces, and seeing the images helps move her mourning process along by making the death "more intelligible" (258).

A few years later, the aftermath of Maricela's death is still felt. Her children still cry, miss their mother desperately, and eagerly visit her grave at the cemetery, which they have to pass every day on the way to school. Vanessa, who is in charge of looking after Maricela's children, is still traumatized by Maricela's death and dreams of her. In some of Vanessa's dreams, Maricela protests that she is still alive, while in the latest dream, she says that she is now fine and at peace.

Vanessa then contacts De León to tell him that they have another family member who is lost in the desert.

Chapter 11 Summary: "We Will Wait Until You Get Here"

The missing relative in question is José Tacuri, who was 15 years old when he left Cuenca for New York. José disappeared in the Arizona desert, just south of Arivaca.

De León attempts to find José by contacting his parents, Gustavo and Paulina, who live in New York and emigrated there to provide for their family. He also interviewed Manny and Felipe, the two teenage cousins José had been travelling with, as well as his family in Ecuador.

José's family and his pregnant girlfriend are in a state of "grief, confusion, and desperation" with regard to the mysteries surrounding José's body (274). It is a state clinical psychologists call "ambiguous loss" and "'is the most stressful loss because it defies resolution and creates confused perceptions about who is in or out of a particular family'" (274). Without having corporeal evidence, the family cannot accept that José may be dead. As De León writes, "if seeing the ravaged body of a person you love is the physical manifestation of Sonoran Desert necroviolence, then having no corpse at all is its spectral form" (266). He contends that:

[T]he Sonoran Desert did what Border Patrol strategists wanted it to do. It deterred José Tacuri from entering into the United States. But instead of just stopping him, the hybrid collectif swallowed him alive, erased all traces of him, and sent shockwaves of grief felt as close as New York City and as far as Ecuador (274).

While José's sister sits in his room and clutches at his clothes, his grandmother still wanders off late at night, looking for him among the local hooligans. His girlfriend vows she will eternally wait for him, confident that they will find some way to be together.

Given that José's parents migrated to New York in the wake of post-9/11 border security, they would not be able to return to Ecuador to visit without risking their safety and permanent deportation. They thus fall into the category of a "permanently settled undocumented population" in the United States: people who cannot risk a visit home but aim to substitute their presence with gifts for their children (270).

Although José's absent parents lavished him with goodies, these were no substitute for their love, and on entering adolescence, José began to rebel. He blamed his parents' abandonment of him for his rebelliousness and told his father "that being reunited with [them] would fill his emptiness inside" (270).

José's journey to the border was relatively uneventful, but once in the desert, he struggled to cope with the heat and having drunk all of his water, and with his electrolytes low, became drowsy. As helicopters began to circulate and catch migrants, the cousins told José that they were going to keep going and left him sitting at the bottom of a hill. That was the last time they saw him, and they are uncertain of what happened to him. José's child, Maria José, was born in November 2013; she is a partial comfort to his family in the wake of his death.

Chapter 12 Summary: "Epilogue"

After weeks of planning, De León arranged for José's mother, Paulina, and the two cousins, Manny and Felipe, who accompanied him across the border, to have an interview with an agent from the Border Patrol's Public Information Office and its Search, Trauma and Rescue Team (BORSTAR). When Manny and Felipe are interviewed by BORSTAR, they "have conflicting accounts regarding how many days they spent in the desert, and their memory of details such as landmarks and cardinal directions they walked are vague" (281). Twelve days after the interview, De León receives an email from BORSTAR stating that they will not continue to search for José, though they think that he likely crossed the boundary east of Sycamore Canyon and separated from his cousins northwest of Atascosa Peak.

In the conclusion to his book, De León takes a look at the factors that would make people such as José and his parents "leave their homes and families to risk life and limb in the desert for the chance to scrub toilets for minimum wage" (283). These include global economic inequality, political instability, war, famine, government corruption, and unregulated capitalism. There are many paths of action that could be taken, such as enforcing a new guest worker program or equalizing trade relations between the United States and Latin America, so that the latter's residents are not so deprived that they feel they have to leave home. De León comes to the conclusion that "the United States' need for cheap labor that can be controlled with the threat of deportation and the duplicitous stance that we don't want undocumented laborers in our country" wins out and stops any real progress (284).

De León recognizes that there is no easy solution to these problems and states that, anyway, this is not the goal of his book, which instead aims to "show the devastating impact that our boundary enforcement system has on people's lives" (284). He has tried to "demystify" the process known as "Prevention Through Deterrence", showing the "complex forms of violence" that arise from it (284). He also intends that his book acts as a testimony for the brave undocumented people who have either made it through the desert or being killed in their attempt to cross it. In providing a space where the general reader can grieve for individuals such as Maricela and José, De León hopes to enshrine a sense of how "our worlds are intertwined and the ethical responsibility we have to one another as humans" (285).

De León is conscious that even as his book goes to press, the perils of undocumented migration and the journeys taken by migrants continue and develop in new ways. More and more Central Americans who are fleeing poverty and violence are joining the masses of migrants who are seeking a new life in the United States. While President Obama, on November 20, 2014 announced an executive action to temporarily stop the deportation of undocumented migrants who arrived in the United States before 2010 or have at least one child who is an American citizen, this has done nothing to help the main actors in De León's book or the 6-7 million undocumented migrants who do not meet the qualifying criteria. It also does nothing to change the way the border is policed or to stop the flow of undocumented migration.

Life continues to be hard for the main actors in the book. Memo and Lucho are continually living in fear of being deported and missing the families they have left behind in Mexico and not seen for twenty years. Christian has suffered an injury that limits his ability to work, but he does his best to earn and send money back to his family. Meanwhile, José's girlfriend, Tamara, is raising their daughter and continues to hope that he will return.

Chapters 8-12 Analysis

In "Perilous Terrain," the final part of his book, De León seeks to show how people who die or disappear in the desert as part of Prevention Through Deterrence are real. They were once very much alive and continue to deeply matter to their families, who will never get over their loss.

Maricela, the woman De León and his students find dead and decomposing in the desert, was a mother of three from Cuenca, Ecuador, who sought to migrate to the United States to secure a better standard of living for her children. In order to identify Maricela, the forensics team had to further deface her body, cutting off her fingers so that they could obtain good prints. Those involved in border enforcement treat Maricela as a statistic—just another body found in the desert that they have to deal with. In front of De León and his students, the senior Border Patrol agent and his two juniors feel awkward in handling Maricela. They make empirical statements about the decomposing body and even joke, saying, "'hopefully, she doesn't burst when we pick her up'" (215). Marcella's body is "'gross'" and abject to the young Border Patrol agent, who acts as though he's dealing with merely a negative side effect of his job (216).

De León shows readers that for Maricela's family, her body is a relic that confirms her death, acts as a site for their grief, and assists them in the mourning process. Both Christian in New York and the relatives in Cuenca ask to see De León's pictures of Maricela in order to view a version of her that is less dismembered than the corpse they receive for the funeral. De León's report of the time he spent with the family and the stories of their grief emphasize the significance of Maricela and the tragedy of her death. She was a woman whose "'dream was to arrive in the United States. She realized her dream, but she died doing it'" (252).

José, a restless 15-year-old who disappeared in the desert on the way to find his parents in New York, was deemed irrecoverable by BORSTAR, who gave up on his case "'after [...] many days analyzing'" the evidence at hand (282). De León shows how José's family are becoming desperate with the lack of evidence of what happened to his body as they restlessly try to recover the facts. Victims of ambiguous loss, having no corpse means that José's family cannot grieve, because "they themselves aren't sure of what has been lost" (275). In showing the disparity between the border officials' treatment of the cadavers or missing bodies of undocumented migrants in the desert and the families' ongoing sense of loss, De León appeals to the readers' sense of pathos and justice: how is it that these people who were fully fleshed members of a family and community were allowed to disappear on American soil?

The final chapters of De León's book, deal with another type of absent presence: that of the parent who migrates illegally to America and leaves their children behind. In the case of Gustavo and Paulina, they knew their children and maintained an economic relationship with them. Despite benefiting from the fruits of their labor, adolescent José felt "*el dolor de dólares*," a pain caused by the replacement of his parents with the gifts they bought him (268).

Sometimes, undocumented benefactors have never met the children they are providing for. For example, Christian, a man who migrated while his girlfriend was pregnant, has never seen his son, nor the house he has bought for his family. Gustavo and Paulina have similarly not met the granddaughter Jose left in his girlfriend's womb before they emigrated. The split families maintain close ties, but De León shows that this comes at a cost to the benefactor, who feels the "tension" from being caught between two disparate worlds and feeling that with the passage of years, they belong properly to neither (236).

In the final section of his book, De León makes it virtually impossible for the reader to not see the human cost of Prevention Through Deterrence. In setting a space where we can "publicly grieve for Maricela, José and the thousands of others who suffer and die as a result of a cruel border policy and a globalized economy that continuously pushes and pulls people to seek work in the United States," we, the reader, are asked to take responsibility for our actions and take ownership of our responsibility to other human beings (285).

CHARACTER ANALYSIS

Jason De León

Jason De León, the author of *The Land of Open Graves*, is currently professor of Anthropology and Chicano/a Studies at the University of California Los Angeles. He is also the Executive Director of the Undocumented Migration Project.

De León acknowledges that being a "male researcher from a working-class Latino background" gives him an advantage in interacting with Latinos on the migrant trail, who are less filtered in their interactions with him, than they may have been with white middle-class researchers (92). De León's background makes him more comfortable with the caustic, sexually-charged *chingaderas* and swearing that his subjects use to tell their stories of desert crossing. Nevertheless, he does not assume that he knows what immigrants are going through as a result of his ethnicity, only that he is in a liminal position between objectivity and subjectivity:

> The tension between my roles as an insider (Latino male) and as an outsider (a university professor) allowed me to share in the 'thickness' of border-crossing culture without foolishly thinking that my ethnicity alone would somehow give me an emic perspective into the desperation required to enter the desert (93).

As a researcher, De León has to allow his subjects to behave as they naturally would as they navigate the migrant trail, recording the details of their journey empirically, and without interfering. Nevertheless, after spending so much time with his subjects, cracking jokes as they navigate the difficulties of the migrant trail, he cannot help but form emotional connections with them. When he sees Memo and Lucho off on their visit to the desert, they remind him to document the moment and De León finds that "it is the first time [he doesn't] want to take any photos" because he is overcome with sadness at the departure of his friends and fears for their lives as they enter the desert with only meager provisions (153). He has to fight to keep from "blubbering," and when Memo and Lucho fail in this particular desert-crossing attempt, De León shares in their devastation and desire to block out difficult feelings with alcohol.

In documenting occasions such as these, where the horrors and disappointments he has witnessed on the migrant trail leave him at the mercy of his emotions, De León models a humane reaction to his readers, one that contrasts with the coldly rational response of many Americans, who numb themselves to the violence and destruction of Prevention Through Deterrence by justifying that the migrants were illegals.

Mike Wells

De León's photographer, Mike Wells, is a consistent if unvocal presence in the book. Wells accompanies De León everywhere, from the Sonora Desert, to the Juan Bosco migrant shelter in Nogales, to the house of Maricela's relatives in Cuenca, Ecuador. His black-and-white photographs provide vital visual accompaniment to De León's descriptions; through them, we can observe the flimsiness of the Sonora Desert portion of the US-Mexico border, which appears as little more than a garden fence. Other photos shows the deformation of migrants' feet after traversing the desert and the unsophisticated kitchen of an impoverished Ecuadorian family, complete with dirt floor and wood fire. In their candid depictions of the arid desert, the violence suffered by migrant bodies, and the poverty that causes people to feel that their homeland can offer them no hope of advancement, Wells's photographs speak to the actions and environments of the world of undocumented migrants.

Memo

To De León, 40-year-old Memo looks like the Mexican comedic actor Cantinflas, because both have "round faces, dark moustaches and contagious smiles" (89). Memo also reminds De León of a beloved but now deceased family member, who had a similar taste for dirty jokes and *chingaderas*. De León and Memo hit it off immediately.

Memo was born in 1969, in a small town on the border of Jalisco and Michoacán, but grew up in Veracruz. He felt compelled to leave because local salaries were low compared to the cost of living. He grew up with "'only [enough] money to eat and barely dress'" himself, and was forced to leave school in fifth grade because he had to work to earn a living (95). Memo was in his twenties, with a broken marriage and two young children, when he made his first border crossing into the United States, with a friend who had a brother-in-law in America.

In the ensuing decades, Memo crossed the border 15 times, picking up low-wage work and "'drinking too much'" (98). Memo's propensity for drink got him into trouble on one occasion, when he was arrested for drunk-driving and deported to Tijuana. He remains determined to cross the border when De León meets him, alongside his staunch buddy, Lucho. Memo feels that the economic conditions in Mexico make it impossible for him to return there, though he does entertain the hope of returning to Mexico and visiting his ailing mother, whom he has not seen for almost twenty years. Struggling to make ends meet in the United States, where he is exploited for cheap labor, Memo's dream of reunion seems like a fantasy. De León uses the determined, wisecracking, yet ultimately tragic figure of Memo, who is trapped by his poverty and permanently estranged from his family in Mexico, to show how even those who survive the challenges of desert life never achieve a truly "'happy ending'" (286). His fate is intended to appeal to the reader's compassion and sense of justice.

Lucho

Memo's friend, Lucho, is a foot taller and twenty pounds lighter than Memo. He is around 47 years old when De León meets him. De León writes that "Lucho is dark-skinned with an unbelievably mellow disposition" and a permanent "slight grin on his face" (90). De León marvels at how Lucho has been able to keep "a perfect set of teeth" and does not show the "physical wear and tear" that one would expect from a 47-year-old who has worked as an undocumented manual laborer in the United States for 30 years and crossed the border multiple times (90). He met his travelling companion and friend Memo in a detention center after he was deported by ICE (Immigration Customs Enforcement).

Lucho has significant family roots in the United States and has lived in Arizona for a long time. He owns a trailer and two cars. He feels compelled to return to the United States because he "'nothing really to go back to'" in Jalisco, Mexico, where he is from (104). When he succeeds in making the final crossing with Memo, he works hard doing "odd jobs and temporary contract work" and continues to "drink heavily" (196). Unlike Memo, whose rendition of the desert-crossing becomes more humorous with the passing of time, Lucho's becomes "serious and morose upon reflection" (197). While a traumatized Lucho determines to never make another journey through the "Arizona wilderness," he "spends a great deal of time looking over his shoulder" for ICE agents who may drag him back through there (286).

Maricela (Carmita Maricel Zhagüi Puyas)

Maricela, the Ecuadorian mother of three who left her family behind in Cuenca to be able to better provide for them, is first introduced as the corpse De León and his students find in the desert. Dressed in camouflage clothing, Maricela is "lying face down in the dirt" as though "she collapsed mid-hike" (210). By the time De León and his students find her in the stages of early decomposition, "rigor mortis has set in and her fingers have started to curl," and she is bloated with post-mortal fluids (210). To the vultures who circle in the air, Maricela is lunch, and to the Border Patrol agents, just another abject illegal migrant body that has to be dealt with.

De León and his photographer, Mike Wells, insist on completing the story of who she is and track down her identification and her family members, who will never be the same after her death. A brave, optimistic character who was determined to go to the United States and send back money to create a better life for her children, Maricela left in pursuit of her "'dream,'" despite her family's protests and fears for her (252).

De León shows the lengths Maricela's family went to in order to find out what happened to her in the desert. The body that was returned to Maricela's relatives in Ecuador was unrecognizable as hers, having "'no face, no hands,'" (256). Its state made it difficult to accept that the corpse really was Maricela. However, upon seeing De León's photographs, Vanessa, Maricela's sister-in-law, feels more at peace for getting closer to the facts of how she disappeared and died. By showing the reader who Maricela was in life, rather than just treating her as a victim of the desert, De León makes it more difficult for the reader to dismiss her as just another illegal who died crossing into a land where she was unwelcome.

José Tacuri

José Tacuri, 15 years old at the time he leaves Cuenca, Ecuador, in order to join his parents in New York, disappears in the Sonora Desert after he manages to successfully cross the border.

De León visits Tacuri's house in Ecuador to find that 15-year-old José has a room "decorated with a combination of items from his fading childhood and his burgeoning adolescence" and dressed in "hip-hop" clothes (265). He looks like "he is posing for the cover of a mix-tape" (265). Feeling "el dolor de *dólares*" after his parents emigrate to New York in order to better provide for the family, and that their gifts were not enough for the emptiness he felt at not seeing his parents, José determines to make the perilous migration journey himself (268).

José arrives to the reader as impetuous and immature, given his acting out and rebelling when his parents leave and his reliance on them for economic support when he has gotten his girlfriend back in Ecuador pregnant. The irresolution of his adolescent state is magnified by his disappearance without a trace in the Sonora Desert, and the family cannot grieve for him because "they will always maintain hope that he is alive" (275).

José's example is important in De León's work because his disappearance without leaving any bodily trace causes the family to suffer "'ambiguous loss,'" a state that creates "'confused perceptions about who is in or out of a particular family'" (274). As traumatic as the recovery of Maricela's remains was for her family, the lack of a body makes it hard for José's family to gain closure, and they find themselves engaging in confused acts, such as looking for him in his old Cuencan haunts. José's example also shows the far-reaching consequences of the Prevention Through Deterrence affect not only the individual concerned, but also their entire family and community.

Christian

A "short raven-haired man in his early thirties," Maricela's brother-in-law, Christian, is a model of "urban Latino fabulousness" in his tight-fitting Abercrombie and Fitch t-shirt and flashy tennis shoes (220). Nevertheless, a story of extreme hardship and hazard belies Christian's slick appearance. As an illegal migrant from Ecuador, Christian endured a perilous and extremely expensive journey to get to the US border, even before he reached the desert. The tribulations of his journey prior to the desert included running through a field of snakes in Costa Rica and exposing himself to a "Mexican hybrid collectif of necroviolence" that greatly endangers Central Americans who attempt to pass through the country in order to reach the United States (229). He was adamant that he did not want Maricela to try her luck at the same journey as him, knowing how hazardous it was.

Christian has left behind his family, including a son he has never met, to reside in Jackson Heights, New York, where he shares an apartment with extended family and a long-term partner. While he is afforded the opportunity to get his

High School Equivalency Diploma and to learn English, Christian "is always cognizant of the high personal cost he has had to pay in order to support his family back in Ecuador" (236). He tries to bridge the two worlds when he saves money, in the hope of getting his ageing parents visas to visit him in New York, along with his 13-year-old son, "whom he has never held in his arms" (286). The precocity of Christian's life in the US is shown when following an injury at work, his coworkers are afraid to call 911, as police may ask for his papers. As a result, he has not received proper medical help for his injury and is limited in the work he can do. Christian's example is yet another in De León's book that shows there are no satisfying resolutions or payoffs for making the life-threatening journey across the desert.

THEMES

Prevention Through Deterrence and the Desert Scapegoat

The premise of De León's book is that the American government and Border Patrol use the Sonora Desert on the US-Mexico border as not only a deterrent for illegal migration but as "a killing field" capable of eviscerating migrant bodies and the evidence that they were there in the first place (8). The government therefore uses the desert wilderness as a scapegoat for the brutal nature of migrant deaths.

De León is keen to show that the Sonora desert, whose "beauty" at sunset is "overwhelming," and which has been viewed as a sacred space by the O'odham desert people, is not the only actor in the death of the migrants who attempt to traverse the border (23). De León makes use of Italian philosopher Giorgio Agamben's "*state of exception*," defined as "the process whereby sovereign authorities declare emergencies in order to suspend the legal protections afforded to individuals while simultaneously unleashing the powers of the state on them" (27). He considers that:

> [L]ike Agamben's characterization of the concentration camp, the spatial arrangement of borders often allows a space to exist outside the bounds of normal state or moral law. Border zones become spaces of exception—physical and political locations where an individual's rights and protections under law can be stripped away upon entrance (27).

It is here, in the Sonora Desert's space of exception, that feats that would be unthinkable in the rest of the country, such as a person dying of dehydration and their remains eaten by vultures, can take place.

De León's project is to render visible what the desert, as employed by the Prevention Through Deterrence's state of exception, threatens to make invisible. He details the bodies of the desert's victims and goes on to provide testimonies of those who have attempted the crossing and either been successful or detained.

Contrasted with the impersonal, federally-imposed scheme of Prevention Through Deterrence, the testimonies of desert-crossers such as Christian, Memo, and Lucho, seem vivid and heroic. Whereas the federal authorities and right-wing media would seek to present the migrants as a faceless swarm of law-breakers, in De León's book, figures such as Memo and Lucho, who have several failed desert-crossing expeditions behind them, become scrupulous, hardy experts who manage to outfox Border Patrol by crossing "in only the most difficult" mountainous areas (195). By giving voice to these migrants' story of determination, ingenuity, and good humor, De León presents Memo and Lucho as idiosyncratic characters who are worthy not only of the reader's attention but of their admiration.

The American Dream of Illegal Border Crossers

De León shows how illegal border crossers harbor the same vision of the American Dream as previous generations of immigrants to the United States. Forced to leave their homes out of economic necessity, they split from their close-knit families and the life they have always known, in search of better wages and opportunities for themselves and their loved ones. Christian, for example, recalls that before he made the journey to America from Ecuador, his family was "'really poor,'" to the point where it was uncertain if they could eat every day (236). He had certain notions of wealth and glamour associated with the United States and was disenchanted with Queens, where his uncle lived, as it was not the "big beautiful buildings in Manhattan and people living the good life," but a place with trash on the street and noise from the train (234).

After settling in Manhattan and being able to send money back, Christian's family could enjoy a greater level of prosperity, including little luxuries, such as the gifts he sent them. On a personal level, Christian feels that his hazardous journey and the ability to make money has made him realize he was "born for a reason and with a purpose," which was to make a different life for himself (236). In working towards his High School Equivalency Diploma and learning English, Christian is moving towards establishing himself as an American, albeit one who is not legally allowed to be there.

De León compares Christian and other illegal border-crossers to previous generations of immigrants from Europe, such as the Irish, who faced terrible prejudice when they arrived during and after the mid-19th-century famine and were exploited for cheap labor. For this reason, he believes in the importance of conserving the material traces of migrant border crossings and gathering the testimonies of those who cross the desert. In doing so, he believes that he is documenting American immigration history for future generations. When *Archeology* magazine published an article about the Undocumented Migration Project, several angry readers wrote to the editor complaining that the article romanticized illegal immigration, with one reader saying:

> '[T]o compare these criminals to the millions of Europeans who immigrated in the late 19th and early twentieth centuries is an insult to their memories and efforts to give their children better lives [...] to document the trash heaps of these current illegal immigrants as artifacts, as if they are sacred, is beyond credibility' (198).

De León feels that such sentiments do not only demonstrate cultural amnesia about the treatment of early European immigrants, but also "illustrates the typical race-based value judgments many make about modern immigration history and contemporary archeological knowledge" (198). Like the previous generations of impoverished, disempowered immigrants, Latinos are needed for their cheap labor and are essential for the running of the American economy; they also possess the American dream of prosperity, freedom, and better opportunities. However, Prevention Through Deterrence, a policy that ruthlessly aims to make entry difficult for them and their illegality once they arrive, prevents them from legitimately writing a new chapter in America's immigration history. De León's project seeks to change both the illegals' voiceless status and the culture that would keep them silent.

Fraternity and Survival on the Migrant Trail

De León writes that "'accidental communit[ies],'" temporary groups formed of people in the same situation, are common on the migrant trail (135). As migrants embark on the perilous cycle of border-crossing, deportation, and preparing to cross again, and face assault by local gangs and drug-dealers, not to mention the Border Patrol, they recognize that "there is strength in numbers" and that it is worth their while to band together with the decent people they encounter on the trail (135). Also, the friendships formed on the trail are a crucial source of emotional support among "'the brotherhood of the defeated,'" poor men who presently "'have very little except each other'" (135).

As the years pass, the cycles of migration—time spent in the United States and deportation—erode traditional family structures, with migrants finding themselves unable to return home and estranged from their families sometimes for decades. This means that the "brotherhood" formed on the trail becomes far more tangible than the men's actual families (135).

Memo and Lucho's friendship, which began in a detention center, is enduring. In the period that De León conducts his research, the two men share time in the Juan Bosco center for deportees and experience two border crossings together, one failed and one successful. Memo and Lucho became *amigos de camino* as their friendship blossoms "over their need to survive deportation to an unfamiliar border town and their shared desire to cross back into the United States," in addition to both men coming from impoverished, working-class backgrounds (94). Most of the time, their ability to joke about the hardships of migration keeps them close; however, after a failed border-crossing and too much to drink, their friendship is put to the test, as Lucho becomes angry and turns on Memo, trying to beat him up. Memo reminds him of their brotherhood and their shared conviction that they must cross the border. Arguably, their solidarity enables them to eventually cross the desert via some of its most perilous terrain.

In larger, less-close-knit communities, it is every man or woman for themselves and loyalties only go so far when crossing the desert. In the case of Maricela and José's crossings, the amply-paid *pasador*, or people-smuggler, was ruthless about leaving struggling people behind, in order to benefit the group as a whole. For example, José, who was travelling with his cousins Felipe and Manny, among others, found himself unable to keep up when he became dehydrated. A guide named Scooby threatened to beat him if he did not get up. While the *pasador's* actions are unmistakably violent, José's weakness compromises the strength of the group and so as in the animal world of travelling herds, José will either have to act in a manner that benefits the border-crossing community or be abandoned by it.

José told his cousins to go and that he intended to turn himself in. The cousins followed Scooby and José was left with the food and water that they gave him. He disappeared and died in the desert. Here, José's teenage cousins had to make the difficult decision to abandon him in order to secure their own advancement. In this example, De León shows how Prevention Through Deterrence puts people in unthinkable circumstances, where they have to provide for their travel companions as best they can and then abandon them to die when they can no longer keep up. In these instances, fraternity breaks down and a sense of individual destiny takes over. In Christian's words, "'they say that everyone has their own luck,'" as to whether they will be strong enough and meet with favorable enough circumstances to survive the desert crossing (237).

SYMBOLS AND MOTIFS

Shoes

Shoes are essential agents for determining whether people will be able to pass through the desert or not. They are a consistent motif in De León's book, a symbol of passing and a barometer of the weathering effects of the desert on migrant bodies. Impoverished border-crossers often do not have state-of-the-art hiking boots and instead make do with the most amenable footwear they are able to afford or get their hands on. The stealing of shoes is a common crime in the Albergue Juan Bosco, where desperate migrants eager to make another crossing, cannot resist taking shoes that are in a better condition than their own. Indeed, in the Albergue, a marker of an untrustworthy person is someone who steals another's shoes and therefore sets back their next attempted crossing.

Shoes often get destroyed beyond the point of usefulness. The state of José's shoes, which are "starting to fall apart," and have "soles [...] coming unglued" is symbolic of the wearer's own physical exhaustion and lack of willpower to carry on with the difficult journey across the desert (272; 273). As De León writes, "those who can't keep up with the a group because of blisters or worn-out shoes are often left behind, which can be a death sentence" (181).

As De León has shown in his own archeological research of abandoned shoes, hardier, more resourceful desert-crossers go to creative lengths to sustain their footwear. For example, in the Tumacáori mountains, De León found a pair of migrant shoes that had been "repaired with a bra strap and cord to attach the soles to the uppers," so that the wearer could keep moving and continue their journey (181). De León applies the archeological concept of *use wear,* a term that refers to "modifications to objects that occur when people use them in various ways," in order to make empirical evaluations of the distress that migrants endure in the desert (181). Unlike blood, vomit, and other bodily fluids, which are eviscerated by the desert within a short time-frame, shoes are more enduring and so can be tangible evidence of the trauma experienced by migrants.

Brown Faces and Bodies

The brown skin color possessed by most Latino migrants is a consistent motif in De León's book; when he refers to migrants both individually and collectively, he emphasizes their skin color, which is different from that of the Anglo-American authorities that would keep them out of the United States.

At the Juan Bosco center for deportees, De León describes how as the police show up, "brown bodies are lined up and frisked" (123). "Brown" empirically describes the general color of the deportees' skin, but because their bodies are referred to in the passive voice, they are disempowered objects, while the police are the active subject. The skin color of the police is not stated and is perhaps left out because they are the ones with the authority and so have the privilege of not being defined by their color.

While De León does not make a specific statement about skin colour, in several places in the text he implies that for many anti-immigration activists, Latinos crossing the US-Mexico border illegally are disanalogous and inferior to the impoverished Europeans who crossed the Atlantic in previous centuries. These anti-immigration activists are thereby making a distinction between the white skin of the Europeans and the brown of the Latinos (198). De León describes anti-immigration activists who make generalizations about Latinos having little care for the natural environment as "racist," and he displays discomfort with the white border agent's abject response to Maricela's brown corpse (191).

De León's counter to the perception of Latino migrants as a conglomerate brown mass is to describe the faces and personalities of the individuals he encounters on the trail in detail, so that they become distinctive characters in the reader's mind, and thereby capable of leading their own narrative. For example, there is "dark-skinned" Lucho, who "always seems to have a slight grin on his face [...] as if he is in on some secret that he wishes he could tell you but can't" (90). In the text, Lucho's distinctive brown face is offered as a sort of preamble to his highly individual story. Thus, his skin color is part of his identity, but not his defining feature.

The Border

The border, a line between the United States and Mexico that is at once real and symbolic, is seen differently by the Border Patrol and the Latino migrants who transgress it. For the Border Patrol, the line is a symbolic fixture that divides American land, terrain that only legal United States citizens should have access to. For Latino border crossers, the border is a surmountable obstacle that stands between them and their dreams. De León even comes across the saying: "'*Para los Mexicanos no hay fronteras.* (For Mexicans there are no borders)'"; it is only a matter of one's body keeping up with one's faith as they make as many attempts as is necessary to get past Border Patrol and the desert (163).

Some American anti-immigration activists believe that the border, which in some places is a flimsy or non-existent, is rather too symbolic, and would reinforce its physicality by building a more substantial structure. For example, Republican Herman Cain proposed a "'real fence [...] twenty feet high with barbed wire. Electrified with a sign on the other side that says, 'It can kill you'" (156). While Cain is in favor of a violently prohibitive structure, De León argues that Prevention Through Deterrence relies on a vaguer idea of the border, whereby the Sonora desert acts as a frontier that exhausts transgressors to death or to the point that they turn themselves in to Border Patrol.

IMPORTANT QUOTES

1. "After spending just a few weeks on the US-Mexico border hanging out with the desperate people looking to breach America's immigration defenses, I quickly learned that death, violence, and suffering are par for the course. It all started to blur together. Disturbing images lost their edge. As an observer, you grow accustomed to seeing people cry at the drop of a hat." (Introduction, Page 1)

   De León sets the scene for—and emotional tone of—his study: a US-Mexico border where devastation and high drama are the norm. He is disturbed by how easily he has become accustomed to the sight of untoward circumstances and people in distress.

2. "This dude had been dead for less than an hour and yet the flies were already there in full force. They were landing on his milky eyeballs and crawling in and out of his open mouth [...] We watched flies lay eggs on this man's face for what seemed an eternity." (Introduction, Pages 2-3)

   In this gruesome portrait of death, De León details what the desert does to the bodies left in it, and his own feelings of powerlessness and horror, as he watches flies make their home in a man's face. Through his use of the colloquialism "dude," De León departs from a formal academic style to convey his very human reaction to the grotesque spectacle he has encountered.

3. "My argument is quite simple. The terrible things that this mass of migrating people experience en route are neither random nor senseless, but rather part of a strategic federal plan that [...] is [...] a killing machine

59

that simultaneously uses and hides behind the viciousness of the Sonoran Desert." (Introduction, Pages 3-4)

Here, De León lays out the book's thesis: that the federal government is using the harsh conditions of the Sonoran Desert as a means of controlling and deterring immigration. Using nature as a foil, the government washes its hands of responsibility to the people killed, as they try to enter the United States.

4. "In my approach to clandestine migration, I have sought to paint crossers not as anonymous shadows scrambling through the desert, but as real people who routinely live and die in this environment and whose voices and experiences we should be privileging." (Introduction, Page 13)

Here, De León sets out his intention to look at the migrants' experiences of the crossing through a lens of humanism. Rather than treating these crossers as anonymous statistics, De León makes a case for respecting their humanity and their own personal narratives of the journey.

5. "For many Americans, this person—whose remains are so ravaged that his or her sex is unknown—is (was) an 'illegal,' a noncitizen who broke US law and faced the consequences. Many of these same people tell themselves that if they can keep calling them 'illegals,' they can avoid speaking their names or imagining their faces." (Chapter 1, Page 26)

Here, De León shows how many Americans use the border crossers' illegality as an excuse to avoid facing the horror that real human beings are dying on the frontiers of their own country. The term "illegals" depersonalizes the border crossers, making them seem like a pest that needs to be controlled.

6. "Many people die in remote areas and their bodies are never recovered. The actual number of people who lose their lives while migrating will forever remain unknown." (Chapter 1, Page 36)

   De León describes the spectral quality of the people who disappear in the desert, never to be seen again. This assists the system that would render their experiences invisible and let the federal government and Border Patrol off the hook.

7. "Prevention Through Deterrence. It has a nice ring to it. It looks good in big bold letters splashed on the front of federal documents. […] It sounds powerful, but not vicious. It wants to convince you that it's a humane policy designed simply to prevent crime, to discourage it before it happens." (Chapter 2, Page 38)

   De León adopts a mocking, propagandistic tone when introducing the reader to Prevention Through Deterrence, the policy that causes the federal government to use the desert as a means of dealing with illegal immigration. He shows how the name makes the government look like a benign agency that is using its country's natural resources to control its borders without much violent interference.

8. "As the desert and all the actants it contains have become incorporated into the Prevention Through Deterrence hybrid collectif, Border Patrol has attempted to separate its policy from the subsequent trauma that migrants experience as a result of being funneled

toward this 'hostile' environment. Rather than being viewed as a key partner in border enforcement strategy, the desert is framed as a ruthless beast that law enforcement cannot be responsible for." (Chapter 2, Pages 42-43)

In this passage, De León exposes Prevention Through Deterrence for the cover-up it is. He shows how the government uses the excuse of a wilderness it cannot control to wash its hands of responsibility for the lives lost on American terrain. In reality, the desert's wilderness fits in with Border Patrol's plan for managing illegal border crossings.

9. "I have read that this is the most humane way to kill a pig in the field. It sure as hell doesn't feel humane. It's also not instantaneous. The animal keeps falling down and getting back up. He walks in half-circles and defiantly refuses to die. 'I gotta do it again,' the gunman tells us. 'His skull is too thick.'" (Chapter 3, Page 62)

The killing of a pig in preparation for De León's experiment to assess the stages of a body's decomposition in the desert is brutal and far from instantaneous. While De León uses a pig because the animal is scientists' preferred proxy for a human body, the violence needed to kill the pig is a foreshadowing of the violence experienced by the humans killed in the desert. It is slow, confusing, agonizing, and gruesome.

10. "Just like the previous two days of feeding, the third starts at daybreak. The difference is that by now the body is a pathetic shell of what it used to be. Even though the bulk of the viscera and muscle were

consumed within the first forty-eight hours, the birds keep working." (Chapter 3, Page 79)

Describing the relentless hunger with which carrion-eaters' peck at the experimental pigs' remains, De León shows the extent of necroviolence that a body left in the desert is subjected to. He also portrays the ruthlessness of nature, where species looks out for its own survival, regardless of the rest, and implicitly draws a parallel with Border Patrol's ability to dehumanize illegal border crossers, who they leave to the predation of nature.

11. "I realized early on that being a male researcher from a working-class Latino background often influenced the ways people interacted with me and how they recounted their crossing stories. Many of the men I spoke to told their hard-luck tales through the lens of *chingaderas* because they knew that I would understand the nuances of this linguistic frame." (Chapter 4, Pages 92-93)

Rather than viewing himself as an impersonal objective researcher, De León is conscious of the figure he cuts among his interviewees. The fact that he is a Spanish-speaking Latino male diminishes the distance between him and his subjects, who feel free to express themselves to him, as they do to each other, through play-routines, or chingaderas.

12. "One of the major misconceptions about immigration control is that if the government spends enough money on fences, drone planes, motion sensors, and Border Patrol agents and makes the crossing process treacherous enough, people will eventually stop coming." (Chapter 4, Page 101)

De León highlights the American government's misguided ideas that technology can prevent immigrants from making the journey across the border. However, even this catalogue of deterrents is no match for immigrants' determination.

13. "They are male, lack formal education, have crossed the border multiple times, and have been incorporated into the US undocumented labor force for years. Both have spent most of their lives living in the United States, and neither sees returning to Mexico as an option." (Chapter 4, Page 106)

    Memo and Lucho's predicament, described here, is "fairly typical" of undocumented border crossers (106). The reader may be surprised to learn that these illegals have spent more time in the country that seeks to discourage them from entering and yet profits from their cheap labor than they have in their homeland.

14. "Like the random events that migrants encounter in the desert that may impede their journey or assist in their success, the criteria Border Patrol used to select the seventy people I am watching being federally prosecuted on this day in Tucson in 2013 are arbitrary. Having your day in court is often just a matter of sheer dumb luck." (Chapter 5, Page 110)

    By likening the randomness of the events that migrants could possibly encounter in the desert with that of having an immigration trial, De León disrupts the illusion that the federal government has control over immigration. The colloquialism "sheer dumb luck" uses ironic humor to demonstrate the lottery-like aspect of border-crossers' fates, not just in the desert, but in the process of deportation.

15. "Like a never-ending scene from Steinbeck's *Tortilla Flat*, every day on *la linea* a drama starring a revolving cast of heroines, hustlers, ne'er-do-wells, and saints plays out on the streets [...] In the same conversation or interaction you can find people weeping and laughing uncontrollably, swearing off the human race and simultaneously being surprised by the kindness of strangers." (Chapter 5, Page 127)

De León portrays la linea, *the narrow strip of land across the border where deportees usually end up, as a place of massive contradictions. This liminal space is a showcase for the best and worst of humanity, where people take advantage of each other and assist each other in close proximity.*

16. "While other customers are buying meat for a Sunday *carne asada*, these guys are shopping for a trip through Hades." (Chapter 6, Page 147)

When De León accompanies Memo and Lucho to the supermarket so they can buy provisions for their trip through the desert, he notes that the grocery store is a regular one and not equipped for epic trips through the Sonora Desert. The juxtaposition of the Mexican Sunday favorite, carne asada, *with the Greek word for the underworld, Hades, highlights the ludicrousness of the men's mission: they are using everyday supplies to attempt the nearly impossible.*

17. "Ex-governor of Arizona and former head of the Department of Homeland Security Janet Napolitano once told a reporter, 'You show me a 50-foot wall and I'll show you a 51-foot ladder at the border.'" (Chapter 6, Page 155)

Napolitano's metaphor of the 50-foot wall and the 51-foot ladder exemplifies the ingenuity and determination of illegal immigrants, who will always find ways to scale a barrier.

18. "Even when their crossing is successful, the event can be traumatic and have lasting emotional, psychological, and physical effects. The act of remembering can conjure pain, fear, and despair. Among American families with undocumented members, it is not uncommon for the topic of their crossing to be a forbidden subject." (Chapter 7, Page 168)

De León feels privileged to hear the tales of migrant crossings of the Sonora Desert because he understands how merely remembering that time can be traumatic for those who have made the journey. Successful border crossers feel that they have to repress their memories of crossing, in order to move on from them and legitimately begin their new lives in America.

19. "An archeological approach can foster engagements with the recent past and its material remains in novel and meaningful ways and produce new information that may be lost in narrative translations of history, collective memories, or accounts of personal experiences." (Chapter 7, Page 172)

De León makes a case for using objects to study migration because they can provide a different type of information than highly-subjective oral histories do. An archeological approach can tell us a lot about how the desert impacts the material aspects of migrants' journey across the desert and can give an empirical indication of how much they have physically endured.

20. "She is wearing generic brown and white running shoes, black stretch pants, and a long-sleeve camouflage shirt. The shirt is something you expect a deer hunter to wear, but over the last several years migrants and drug mules have adopted the fashion. The brown and green design blends perfectly with the Sonoran backdrop this time of year." (Chapter 8, Page 210)

When De León finds Maricela's corpse, it is expertly outfitted in clothing that is suitable for being camouflaged in the desert. The tragic irony is that while Maricela was able to hide from Border Patrol, her abandonment and death in the desert threatened to camouflage, if not eradicate, her story. It is also poignant that given her scrupulous preparations for the crossing, she did not make it.

21. "The deaths that migrants experience in the Sonoran Desert are anything but dignified. That is the point. This is what 'Prevention Through Deterrence' looks like. These photographs should disturb us, because the disturbing reality is that right now corpses lie rotting on the desert floor and there aren't enough witnesses." (Chapter 8, Page 213)

When De León is told that his photographs of Maricela's corpse robbed her of her dignity, he retorts by saying that exposition of the indignity of dying in the desert is his point. De León urges the reader to witness the horror in the photographs and experience all the natural human reactions of witnessing a corpse in the desert.

22. "Central and South American migrants, who accounted for 31 percent of all people deported by the US federal

government in 2013 [...] pass through multiple borders using a variety of transportation methods. This includes walking or running for their lives, crossing rivers on rafts, and riding on the tops of freight trains, all before arriving at the US-Mexico boundary for the chance to try their luck in the desert." (Chapter 9, Page 222)

De León shows that the journey taken by Central and South Americans is especially epic, as they have to face many dangers even before encountering the Sonora Desert. It makes the success of those like Christian seem especially miraculous, and paints a picture of the determination these migrants have to enter the United States and make a better life for themselves.

23. "'She always said she had to get there. [...] Her dream was to arrive in the United States. She realized her dream, but she died doing it.'" (Chapter 10, Page 252)

Deceased Maricela's sister-in-law, Vanessa, says how Maricela had her own version of the American Dream: to arrive in America and provide for her family, so they could enjoy a better standard of living. However, the tragedy was that because of Prevention Through Deterrence, she paid for that dream with her life.

24. "José's room looks like a lot of other teenagers' rooms. The only difference is that this place is frozen in time. Nothing here has moved since he left for the United States and disappeared in the Arizona desert just south of Arivaca." (Chapter 11, Page 265)

After a detailed description of missing José's room, De León concludes that it is the space of a regular teenager. However, its eerie time-capsule-like quality, which De León later likens to a cenotaph, indicates his family's inability to accept his loss. They keep his room as he left it, in case he somehow returns.

25. "In some ways, though, this book is also a testimony given by survivors of the Sonoran Desert hybrid collectif and an obituary for those who succumb to it. The words, stories and images that the undocumented people in the preceding pages have allowed me to share are their public declarations that their lives are worth noting, valuing and preserving." (Chapter 12, Page 284)

    De León concludes his book by emphasizing that the people whose stories he uses as evidence, are at the center of its project. By giving space to the voiceless, who the Sonoran Desert collectif would obliterate, he intends that the reader will empathize with them and value their contribution, both in terms of their narratives and their lives.

ESSAY TOPICS

1. Describe the features of Prevention Through Deterrence. How does De León show that the policy is not as benign as it initially appears?

2. Discuss the role of emotion and empathy in De León's book. Why do you think that De León seeks to appeal to the reader's emotions as well as to their logic?

3. What role do friendship and solidarity play in migrants' journeys across the border?

4. What case does De León make for an archeological approach to learning about migrant experiences in the Sonora Desert? What do you view as the strengths and limitations of this approach?

5. How does De León's status as a male Latino researcher from a working-class background influence his relationships with the people he meets on the trail?

6. How do illegal Latino migrants compare with previous generations of immigrants to the United States? In what ways is there controversy around this issue?

7. Describe the differences in American and Latino perceptions of the border between the United States and Mexico.

8. Discuss De León's depiction of violence. What forms does it take in the narrative and how does Prevention Through Deterrence disguise it?

9. In what ways does De León show how family life is impacted by illegal migration to the United States?

10. What techniques does De León use to privilege the voices of migrants and why is this so important to his project?

Made in United States
North Haven, CT
28 March 2022